The Candlestick Manual for Traders

A Hands-On Guide to Analyzing Price Action and Executing Profitable Trades with Confidence

by

Nathaniel J. Brooks

DISCLAIMER

This book is only designed for educational and informational purposes. It is intended to illustrate trading ideas, systems, and market insights gained through study and practice. It is not designed to provide personalised financial guidance or suggestions.

This book does not provide any financial, investing, legal, or trading advice. All techniques, charts, examples, and scenarios are offered solely for educational illustration and should not be regarded as recommendations to buy, sell, or hold any financial asset.

Trading in the foreign exchange market and other financial instruments entails risk, including the loss of funds. No method, strategy, or example presented in this book can guarantee success. Market conditions vary, and previous performance is no guarantee of future results or illustrations.

Readers are solely responsible for their trading decisions, risk management, and outcomes. Trading should only be done with funds that you can afford to lose. Readers are encouraged to seek financial expert guidance as needed.

All chart drawings in this book are based on publicly available market price data and are intended solely as analytical examples for educational purposes. Charts, tools, platforms, brokers, and software are only mentioned for instructional purposes. The author is not

Table of Contents

INTRODUCTION

Why Candlesticks Matter

There's a point in every trader's journey where you stop chasing the next best indicator and start asking a deeper question: *What is the market really doing right now?*

I came to that point the hard way. My charts used to look like a spaceship control panel, colorful indicators layered one on top of another, each promising to tell me when to buy or sell. Moving averages, RSI, stochastic oscillators, even custom scripts I downloaded from forums. I followed them religiously. And yet, my trades kept going wrong.

I wasn't clueless. I understood how those tools worked. But they were always late. By the time an indicator gave a signal, the move had already started, or worse, it was already fading. It felt like trying to steer a car by looking in the rearview mirror.

One day, I removed everything. No indicators, no signals. Just candlesticks on a clean chart. It felt uncomfortable at first, like stepping into the market naked. But something in me knew that the answers I was chasing might be in the raw price itself.

That day marked the beginning of a turning point in my trading career.

What I didn't realize then, and what you might be about to discover, is that **candlesticks tell a story**. Each one reflects a mini-battle between buyers and sellers. It shows who's winning, who's struggling, and when momentum is shifting. Over time, I learned that you don't need complicated tools to find trades. You need **clarity**, and candlesticks provide exactly that if you know how to read them.

In this book, I'm going to walk you through the entire blueprint that helped me and many others turn confusion into control. Whether you're brand new to trading or someone who's been at it for a while without consistent results, this guide is written for you. It doesn't matter how experienced you are, what matters is that you're ready to understand price in a way that cuts through the noise.

You're going to learn how candlesticks work, how to spot key patterns, and more importantly, how to interpret them in **real-time market conditions**. Not just in hindsight or textbooks, but in the heat of the moment, when a new candle forms, and you're deciding whether to enter, hold, or exit.

Let me be honest with you: trading isn't easy. If it were, everyone would be doing it successfully. What makes it hard isn't the market. It's the mind, the emotions, the doubt, the overthinking. You can have the right setup and still lose money if you don't understand what you're seeing. That's why learning how to read candlesticks is so powerful. It gives you a lens to see through the chaos.

I remember one day, back when I was still refining my approach, I spotted a textbook bullish pin bar forming near a key support zone on the GBP/USD chart. Every part of me wanted to enter the trade immediately. But something didn't sit right. The volume was dropping, and the preceding candles lacked conviction. I waited.

Ten minutes later, the next candle invalidated the signal. It turned out to be a false move, one that would've cost me had I jumped in too early. That's the kind of clarity candlestick reading gives you. It's not just about spotting patterns. It's about understanding **context**, and learning to trust what the candles are showing you instead of what you hope will happen.

You'll come across patterns like engulfing candles, inside bars, pin bars, and more, but what matters is *where* they show up, *when* they appear, and *what story they tell in relation to the overall market structure.* A bullish engulfing candle in a downtrend doesn't mean the market is ready to reverse. It might be a trap. But that same candle at a strong demand zone, with confluence from support and a slowing bearish push? That's a different story.

We'll go deep into all of this. We'll also talk about risk, trade management, and how to develop a practical strategy you can use with confidence, even on volatile days when the market seems unpredictable.

If you've ever placed a trade and stared at it nervously, wondering if you made the right choice, you're not alone. I've been there more times than I can count. And I'm telling you, you can get to a place where you feel calm, in control, and fully aware of what's unfolding on your screen. It's not about predicting the future. It's about reading the **present** with skill.

You'll also learn from my past trades, both the wins and the losses. I won't sugarcoat anything. Some of the best lessons I've learned came from bad entries, misread patterns, or rushing into setups without waiting for confirmation. These stories aren't just meant to entertain you, they're meant to remind you that mistakes are part of the learning curve, and you're not alone in making them.

This isn't about trading full-time or chasing fast profits. It's about building a skill that you can rely on for the long run. Candlestick trading, when done right, is clean, efficient, and powerful. You'll need to practice. You'll need to journal your trades, track your progress, and constantly refine your decision-making. But the payoff is real: clarity, control, and confidence.

The rest of this book will guide you step-by-step, from the basics of candlestick structure to crafting a full strategy you can call your own. Each chapter builds on the last, using simple explanations and real-world examples so you can apply what you're learning without guessing.

So, here's my honest offer: I'll bring the knowledge, the experience, and the stories. You bring your focus and your willingness to grow. Together, we'll break down the candlestick blueprint, one chapter at a time.

Let's begin.

CHAPTER 1

The Language of the Market – What Candlesticks Really Tell You

Every movement on a price chart has a meaning. You're not just looking at lines or candles filling the screen. You're watching how money flows in and out of the market, how traders react to levels, and how fear and greed play out in real-time. When you start treating candlesticks as expressions of crowd behavior, everything becomes clearer.

You might have seen candlesticks before and thought they looked like just another way to display price. That's how I used to feel too. It wasn't until I started trading full-time and removed most of my indicators that I finally saw what candlesticks were really showing me. They're not just visual markers. They're **messages from the market**, and once you understand their structure, you'll begin to recognize what traders are doing behind the scenes.

What a Single Candlestick Reveals

Every candlestick contains four key pieces of information: the opening price, closing price, high, and low for a specific time period. It's simple in theory, but packed with insight.

When the close is higher than the open, the candle is typically bullish, meaning buyers were stronger during that period. If the close is lower than the open, it's bearish, sellers were more aggressive. But what truly matters is **how the candle formed** and **where** it formed.

Long wicks, short bodies, strong closes, indecision candles, all of these tell you something different. A long upper wick with a small body near the bottom shows rejection. A small candle after a strong move might hint at a slowdown. A large, full-bodied candle breaking through a key level is often a sign of commitment.

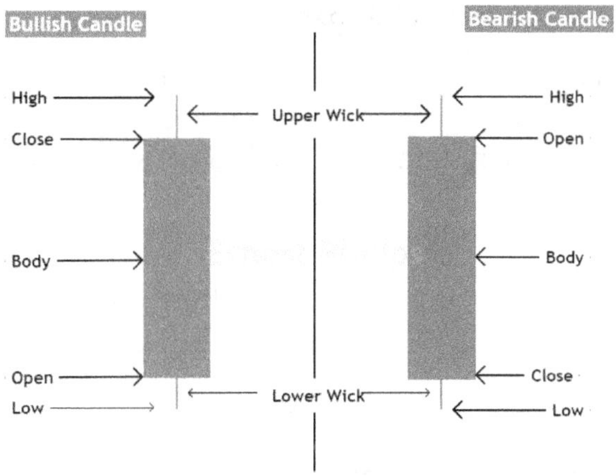

Chart 1: A side-by-side comparison of bullish and bearish candlesticks showing the open, close, high, and low

The Importance of Context

You can't read candlesticks in isolation. One candle means little unless you understand its surroundings. Think of each candlestick as a single word. It's only when you read several of them together that you begin to understand the full message.

When I started noticing patterns like a bullish engulfing candle forming after a series of small bearish candles at a support zone, it finally clicked. The structure told me buyers were stepping in at a price level they believed was too cheap. That wasn't just a pattern, it was a shift in power.

You'll see patterns repeat, but they don't always mean the same thing. A hammer candle at the top of a trend doesn't mean what it means at the bottom. Location matters. What comes before and after the candle matters even more.

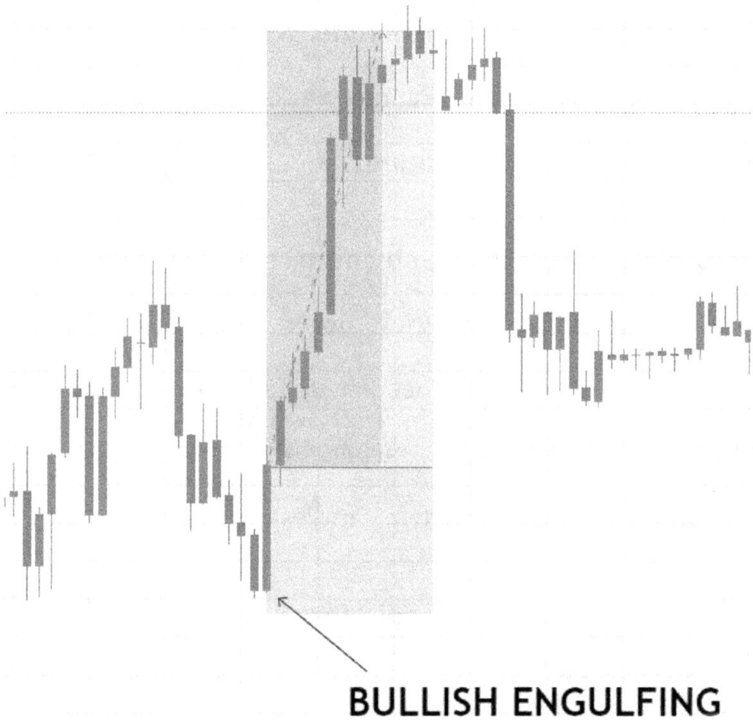

Chart 2: GBP/USD H4 showing a bullish engulfing candle near a demand zone

Why Candlesticks Beat Indicators

Indicators lag. They follow what's already happened. Candlesticks happen in real time. When you watch how a candle builds, when it hesitates, wicks out, or breaks clean, you get clues that no indicator can match.

I used to rely heavily on moving averages. They smoothed the trend, sure. But they never told me what was *happening right now*. Once I switched to reading candles, I started catching moves earlier. I didn't need to wait for confirmation that came five candles too late.

This isn't about bashing indicators. They can support your analysis. But your first layer should always be **price itself**, and candlesticks are the clearest way to read price.

The Anatomy of Momentum and Reversal

Momentum is visible through strong, continuous candles with little to no wick. Reversals tend to start with hesitation, candles get smaller, wicks get longer, and direction changes slowly before a full reversal candle confirms the shift.

Let's say the market's been trending down. Then you get a doji, a candle with nearly equal open and close, followed by a strong bullish candle that closes above the previous highs. That sequence tells you sellers are losing grip and buyers are moving in with conviction.

Understanding this rhythm takes time, but it's the key to finding clean trades without relying on guesswork.

Chart 3: GBP/USD D1 chart showing a downtrend that pauses, forms a inverted hammer, and reverses with a bullish engulfing.

When Candlesticks Lie

Not every candle tells the truth. Some moves are fakeouts. You might see a breakout candle that looks strong, only to find it was a trap, and price snaps back immediately. That's why **volume, market session, and surrounding structure** matter.

One of my biggest early losses came from trading a breakout candle during low-volume hours. The move looked clean. Big bullish candle, clean break above resistance. I jumped in. Ten minutes later, price reversed sharply. What I didn't notice was the lack of follow-through and the fact that the move happened right before market close.

That trade taught me to always read more than the candle.

Final Thoughts for the Chapter

Learning to read candlesticks isn't about memorizing patterns. It's about recognizing pressure. You're observing how buyers and sellers respond to key levels, how momentum builds or fades, and how human behavior unfolds on the screen.

You'll get it wrong sometimes. You'll enter too early, misread a wick, or exit just before the move happens. I've done all of that. But each mistake sharpens your eye. And with every new chart you read, you'll start to see what most traders miss.

Start watching your candles closely. Let them speak before you act. Eventually, you won't need confirmation from anywhere else.

In the next chapter, we'll explore how to identify **high-probability candle setups**, the ones that consistently appear before strong moves, and how to spot them early, in live market conditions.

CHAPTER 2

High-Probability Candle Setups That Signal Strong Moves

If you've ever felt unsure about when to enter a trade, you're not alone. One of the biggest challenges traders face is knowing when a candle actually means something versus when it's just noise. Price moves up and down all day, but not every move deserves your attention. What separates a random flicker from a meaningful signal is **structure, timing, and context**.

In this chapter, you'll learn to recognize **high-probability candlestick setups** that tend to occur before solid market moves. These are the same types of patterns I've seen play out again and again across all major forex pairs. And while no pattern is perfect, these setups, when combined with proper analysis, can boost your decision-making in a big way.

The Engulfing Candle Setup

An engulfing candle happens when the current candle fully covers the previous one, body and sometimes even wicks. If the market has been trending in one direction, and suddenly a candle closes strongly in the opposite direction, engulfing the last one, that's often a signal of shifting control.

Let's say the price has been making lower highs and lower lows. You then spot a bullish candle that completely swallows the prior bearish one. That's not just a coincidence. It often shows that buyers have stepped in aggressively and that momentum could be turning.

I once used this setup during a live GBP/USD trade on the 1-hour chart. Price had dropped steadily for hours, but when it reached a historical support zone, I noticed a bullish engulfing candle form, and it wasn't just any engulfing. It closed above the last two candles, signaling strong rejection. I entered with a tight stop below the candle's low. That trade ran for over 90 pips before stalling.

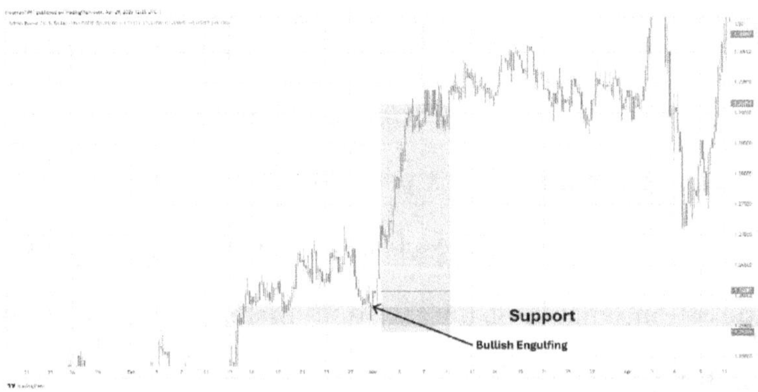

Chart 4: GBP/USD H1 chart showing a bullish engulfing candle forming at a prior support zone, breaking through the structure with volume

The Pin Bar Reversal Setup

A pin bar is a candle with a long wick and a small body, usually formed after a strong directional move. When a pin bar appears at a key level, support, resistance, or a trendline, it often shows rejection of price and can signal a reversal or temporary pullback.

But context is everything. A bullish pin bar in the middle of nowhere means little. Place that same pin bar near a support zone that's been tested before, and now you're reading something real.

A student of mine once showed me a trade he was hesitant to take. It was on EUR/USD. The price approached a resistance zone it had tested twice already. As the third touch happened, a sharp wick punched through the level but closed lower, leaving a clean bearish pin bar. That candle told the whole story. Price couldn't stay above resistance, and sellers were pushing it down hard.

He took the short and exited with 1:3 R:R. It wasn't a gamble, it was a calculated move backed by structure and candlestick behavior.

Chart 5: EUR/USD H4 chart showing a bearish pin bar at a resistance zone after two previous touches

Inside Bars and Consolidation Breakouts

Inside bars are candles that stay completely within the range of the previous candle. They don't break the high or low of the one before them, which means **the market is pausing**. This often happens before breakouts, especially during trending markets.

When you see an inside bar at the end of a pullback, especially after a clean directional push, it's often worth watching closely. It shows indecision or tight compression before price decides where to go next. And when that breakout happens, it can lead to sharp continuation moves.

On the AUD/USD chart, I've used inside bar breakouts to catch short momentum trades. The trick is not to assume direction. Let the market break first, then enter with the trend. This approach avoids getting trapped by false moves.

Avoiding Traps: When a Setup Isn't Enough

There will be days when you see a perfect engulfing candle, or a textbook pin bar, and the trade still fails. That's part of the process. A high-probability setup doesn't guarantee a win, it simply increases your odds.

I've had trades where everything lined up technically, but the timing was wrong. It was a slow session, or news was due in twenty minutes. In those moments, what looks ideal on the chart can become dangerous in practice.

That's why you should always tie your setups to market context. Is this setup forming near a clean level? Is the trend clear? Is the session active? Did the candle form with strength, or did it barely move?

The more questions you ask before entering, the more confident you'll feel placing the trade.

Conclusion: Build Confidence Through Repetition

You don't need to memorize 20 candle patterns to succeed. What you do need is a clear understanding of a few **reliable setups**, and how they behave in different market conditions. The best traders don't chase complexity, they master the simple things.

Start tracking these setups in your charting journal. Note the ones that worked, and the ones that didn't. Over time, your brain will start picking them out faster, and your confidence will grow.

In the next chapter, we'll talk about how to combine candlestick setups with **key support and resistance zones**, so your entries become even more precise and logical. That's where structure starts working hand-in-hand with price action to give you cleaner trades and tighter risk.

Keep it simple. Stay patient. Let the candles guide you.

CHAPTER 3

Support and Resistance – How Structure Enhances Candle Signals

Once you start seeing candlestick patterns clearly, the next step is knowing **where** they matter. A bullish engulfing candle in the middle of a range means almost nothing. But when that same candle forms at a well-tested support level, the story changes. This is where structure steps in to support the message.

Support and resistance aren't magic lines. They're areas where buyers or sellers have previously made strong decisions. These zones show where traders have historically reacted, and that reaction can often repeat.

Understanding Key Zones on the Chart

Support is a level where price tends to stop falling and may reverse upward. Resistance is where price usually stops rising and may turn back down. These levels are shaped by previous highs, lows, consolidations, or breakout points. They act like psychological markers, traders notice them, even if they're using different strategies.

When you place a candlestick setup on top of a key support or resistance zone, it gives the pattern meaning. A pin bar rejecting a support line after a downtrend tells a stronger story than the same pin bar forming in the middle of nowhere.

One thing I often do when marking these zones is zoom out on a higher timeframe. You may see a cluster of wicks rejecting the same level on the 4-hour or daily chart. That's a sign that traders are defending that price. Then, when you switch back to a lower timeframe, you wait for a candlestick pattern at that level to signal your entry.

Chart 6: EUR/USD H4 chart with horizontal support and resistance zones marked from previous swing highs and lows.

The Role of Confirmation at Structure Levels

You don't always want to jump into a trade the moment price touches support or resistance. Instead, watch how price behaves there. Candles that show rejection, hesitation, or strong commitment at these levels are your confirmation.

Let's say price approaches resistance with a few weak bullish candles. Suddenly, a strong bearish engulfing candle appears. That single candle, forming right at the level where sellers previously stepped in, could be your sign to go short.

I've missed great setups in the past by rushing in before seeing confirmation. Once I started combining price structure with candle confirmation, my win rate increased. It wasn't because I found a new pattern. I simply started being patient enough to **wait for the market to tell me** what it wanted to do.

Support Becomes Resistance and Vice Versa

One of the most useful concepts you'll come across is the idea of **role reversal**. When price breaks above a resistance level and then returns to retest it, that resistance often becomes support. The same works the other way around.

These are the areas where some of the cleanest trades form, especially if you're using candlesticks for confirmation. After a breakout, the market often pulls back to retest the level. If a bullish pin bar or engulfing candle forms during that retest, it shows that traders are stepping in to defend the new zone.

During a USD/CHF trade I took last year, I watched resistance turn into support on the 1-hour chart. After price broke out cleanly, I waited. The retest happened a few hours later. A pin bar with a long lower wick formed right on the old resistance line. That entry ran nearly 100 pips with minimal drawdown.

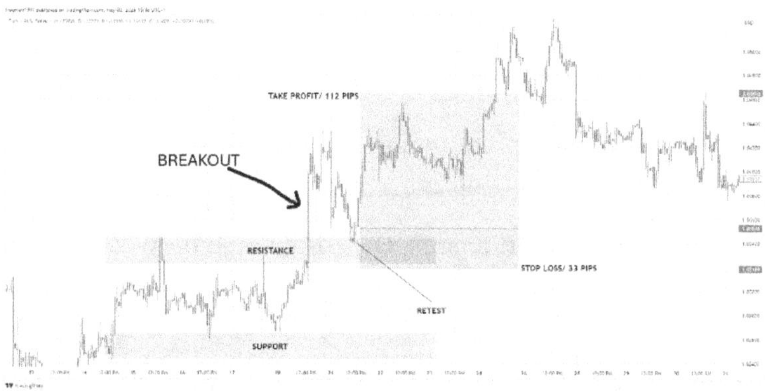

Chart 7: EUR/USD H1 chart showing a clean breakout above resistance followed by a pullback and bullish pin bar confirmation at the new support

Wicks, Closes, and Candle Bodies at Key Levels

It's not just the presence of a candle at a structure level that matters, it's how the candle behaves. If a candle's wick pierces through support but the body closes above, that suggests rejection. On the other hand, a candle with a full body closing below support might signal a stronger breakdown.

Pay attention to the **closes** of candles. They show where the market finally settled after the back-and-forth. Wicks tell you what was tested. Bodies tell you who won. Together, they help you gauge conviction.

In many of my own trades, the difference between a good and bad entry came down to whether the **candle closed** below or above the zone. You'll learn to wait for the close instead of reacting too early. That simple habit could save you from multiple failed trades.

Fine-Tuning Entry Precision with Candle and Structure

When price forms a strong candle setup at a well-respected level, you can act with more confidence. You're no longer guessing. You're aligning market behavior with history.

Sometimes you'll see false breakouts, price moves slightly beyond a level and then snaps back. These moves often trap inexperienced traders. But if you wait for a clean candle close and some rejection, you avoid being on the wrong side of those traps.

Combining structure with candlestick analysis makes your trading tighter. You stop chasing trades in the middle of ranges and start focusing on clean, focused areas where price makes real decisions.

Final Thoughts for the Chapter

You've now seen how structure, support and resistance, adds clarity to candlestick setups. It's not enough to spot a pattern. You need to know **where** that pattern is forming and what traders are likely thinking around that level.

This combination of levels and candles forms the core of technical trading. It's how experienced traders keep things simple without relying on dozens of indicators. You'll see it more clearly the more you mark up charts, observe reactions, and track how candles behave at meaningful levels.

In the next chapter, we'll go deeper into **trend reading**, and how candles help confirm the strength or weakness of a market direction. When combined with structure, trend gives you a powerful framework for consistent day trading.

CHAPTER 4

Reading the Trend with Candlesticks

Understanding market direction is at the heart of every successful trade. It's not enough to identify a bullish or bearish candlestick pattern, you need to know whether the market is moving with or against you. This is where trend recognition becomes your strongest ally.

You may have found a strong pin bar or an engulfing pattern, but if it's fighting against a dominant trend, the probability of success drops. When I started taking trend context seriously, my charts became easier to read, and more trades started working out with less stress.

Defining the Trend in Simple Terms

A trend is just the market moving in one direction for a period of time. If price keeps making higher highs and higher lows, it's trending up. If it forms lower highs and lower lows, that's a downtrend. When there's no clear movement either way, the market is said to be ranging.

Candlesticks help you confirm these movements visually. You can read the conviction of buyers or sellers through the size of the candles, how they close, and how they respond to previous candles. This gives you an ongoing story of what the market participants are doing.

Trends don't always move in straight lines. There will be retracements, pauses, and sometimes even traps. That's why you need more than just a quick glance to read them accurately. A sequence of strong bullish candles followed by a minor pullback usually tells you that buyers are still in control.

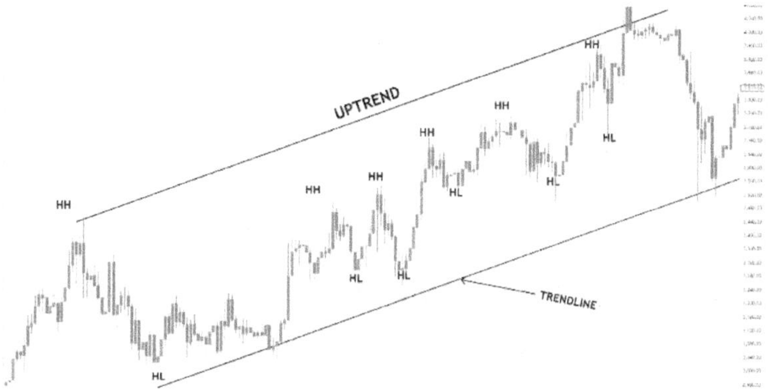

Chart 8: GBP/USD H1 chart showing a clear uptrend with higher highs and higher lows.

Using Candlestick Clues to Validate Trend Strength

Not all trends are created equal. Some are aggressive, while others crawl along. The candles tell you how committed the buyers or sellers are. In a strong bullish trend, you'll often see large green candles closing near their highs, with shallow retracements. In a weak trend, the candles may have long wicks or close with indecision.

Sometimes, traders get confused when they see alternating candles, one bullish, one bearish, forming in a trending market. But if the overall structure is still intact, that's often just a pullback or consolidation, not a reversal.

I used to misread these situations a lot. I'd assume a reversal was forming when it was just a pause. But after spending more time reviewing past trades and candle behavior, I started spotting the difference between weakness and natural rest. Once you develop that sensitivity, you'll feel more at ease waiting for proper setups.

Identifying Trend Reversals Through Candle Signals

Even the strongest trends eventually end. The key is knowing when momentum is fading and when a reversal may be taking shape. Candlestick patterns offer early signs, especially when the candles start to lose size, show rejection wicks, or close opposite to the prevailing direction.

Let's say you're in a downtrend and you begin to see multiple small-bodied candles with long lower wicks. Then suddenly, a bullish engulfing candle appears and closes above the previous high. That's a warning sign. The sellers are no longer in control, and buyers are stepping in.

Reversals often start at key structure levels. If a trend approaches a major support or resistance and starts forming rejection candles or engulfing patterns in the opposite direction, it may be signaling a shift. Still, patience is critical, wait for strong confirmations.

Avoiding the Trap of Trading Against the Trend

One of the quickest ways to damage your trading confidence is by constantly trying to call tops or bottoms. It feels exciting when you catch one right, but most of the time, you're swimming against the current.

Even if you spot a valid pattern, trading against the trend puts you at a disadvantage. You may get stopped out quickly, or the move may lack momentum. A better approach is to wait for pullbacks and look for entries in line with the larger direction.

I've had my fair share of losses trying to "outsmart" the market. I'd enter based on what I *wanted* to see, not what was truly there. With time, I realized I didn't need to fight the trend to be profitable. I just needed to align with it and wait for the right moments.

When to Use Lower Timeframes for Trend Confirmation

Sometimes the trend is clear on a higher timeframe but looks messy on a smaller one. That's normal. What you're seeing is noise, short-term price action that hasn't yet aligned with the bigger move.

In these situations, let the higher timeframe guide you. Use the lower timeframe only for entries. You might see a pullback forming, and then a clean candle setup aligning with the higher trend. That's often your best chance for a low-risk, high-probability trade.

Conclusion of the Chapter

Reading the trend with candlesticks goes beyond simply identifying direction. It's about understanding the pace, strength, and conviction behind each move. When you align your trades with the flow of the market, your setups become more reliable and less stressful to manage.

Candlesticks reveal the mood of the market, whether it's determined, hesitant, or shifting. Combine that with trend recognition, and your decision-making gains clarity. The more charts you study, the more fluent you become in this visual language.

In the next chapter, we'll shift to a deeper breakdown of specific candlestick patterns and how to apply them in real-world trading environments. It's not just about spotting them, it's about timing, structure, and how the market builds the setup before your eyes.

CHAPTER 5

Mastering Reversal Patterns

Knowing when a market is about to turn can be a powerful edge. Reversal patterns don't just mark the end of a trend; they often signal the beginning of fresh trading opportunities. You don't need to catch every top or bottom, but when you understand what a genuine reversal looks like, you'll stop falling for false moves.

I used to take every bullish pin bar at support or every bearish engulfing near resistance as a guaranteed reversal. The losses piled up until I realized the context was missing.

It's not about finding patterns, it's about understanding them in the flow of price action.

What Makes a Reversal Pattern Work

A reversal pattern isn't just a few candles lined up in a fancy shape. For it to matter, it has to show a true change in momentum. You're watching for moments when buyers lose their grip after dominating the chart, or when sellers finally get exhausted and can't push lower anymore.

The clearest signs come when a strong trend starts showing hesitation. You might see smaller candle bodies, rejection wicks forming more frequently, or a shift in how price closes. Then, a decisive candlestick appears, like an engulfing candle, piercing pattern, or a strong pin bar. These aren't just patterns; they're signals that sentiment is changing.

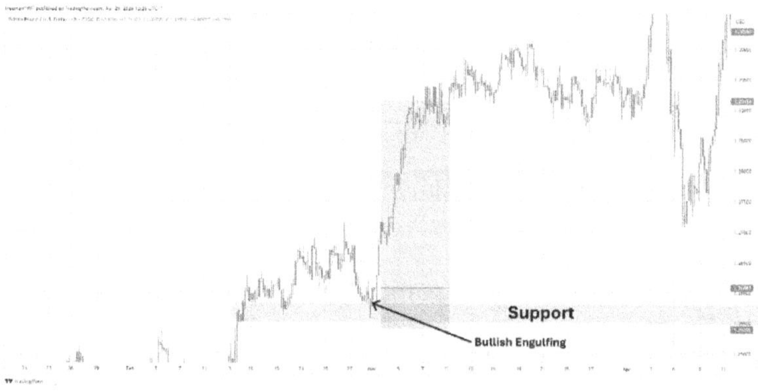

Chart 9: GBP/USD H4 chart showing a downtrend ending with a bullish engulfing candle at a support zone.

High-Probability Bullish Reversal Patterns

A few patterns show up repeatedly on forex charts when a bullish reversal is forming. One of the most reliable is the bullish engulfing. It happens when a large bullish candle fully engulfs the body of the previous bearish one, especially after a series of lower lows.

Another pattern that tends to work well is the hammer. It has a small body near the top with a long lower wick. The wick shows strong rejection of lower prices, and when it forms after a downtrend, it often leads to a shift in direction, if it's at a key level.

In my experience, the strongest bullish reversals happen at areas of previous support or zones where price stalled before. You'll recognize them more clearly when you stop scanning for perfect shapes and instead start asking what the candle behavior tells you.

Key Bearish Reversal Patterns to Learn

When a bullish run gets exhausted, you'll see price slowing down. If you notice a shooting star, where the upper wick is long and the body is small, it signals rejection of higher prices. This doesn't mean jump in blindly, but it's a red flag that buyers are losing steam.

Another strong bearish reversal is the bearish engulfing candle. If a large red candle fully covers the previous bullish body and it forms near resistance or at the end of a strong push, it often means sellers are stepping in with force.

The same rules apply here, location matters. If the pattern shows up in the middle of a trend with no strong structure nearby, it's more likely to fail. What you want to see is the reversal happening after a clear run, preferably near a zone where price turned in the past.

How to Confirm a Reversal Pattern

One pattern by itself rarely tells the full story. To increase your chances, you need confirmation. That might come in the form of a break of structure, like when price breaks a trendline or creates a lower low after a bullish run.

Volume can help in some cases, though not all traders use it in forex. What always helps, though, is observing how the next few candles behave. If you get a bearish reversal pattern and the next candle is another strong bearish close, that's your follow-through.

Confirmation also comes from confluence. If you've got a key support or resistance level, a reversal pattern, and perhaps a Fibonacci level lining up, that setup becomes much stronger.

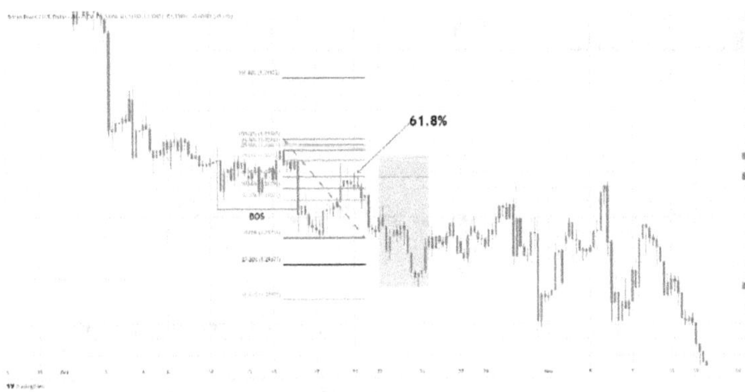

Chart 10: GBP/USD 4Hour chart showing a bearish pin bar forming near the 61.8% Fibonacci level with follow-through.

When Reversal Patterns Fail

Even with the best setups, not every reversal pattern will work. There are times when the market looks ready to turn, but then it breaks straight through. That's why risk management exists, because no pattern offers certainty.

You might have seen a clean pin bar, waited for the next candle to confirm, entered your trade, and then the market ignored it completely. It happens. What you don't want to do is chase the same idea again out of frustration.

When I first started, I would take every failed pin bar personally. Over time, I realized I needed to look at failed reversals as part of the job. They can even offer clues. If a strong pattern fails, it sometimes means there's deeper momentum in play, and that can point to a bigger breakout in the opposite direction.

Conclusion of the Chapter

Reversal patterns, when used with candlestick analysis and proper context, offer a powerful window into the market's shift in direction. You don't need to predict every top or bottom. You just need to learn what genuine shifts look like and wait for those moments.

The more you study these patterns, especially on key levels, the clearer they become. They stop looking like drawings in a textbook and start feeling like natural pauses or turns in price movement. With time, your eyes begin to catch them without second-guessing.

In the next chapter, we'll move deeper into continuation patterns. These help you stay with a winning trend and add more confidence when it looks like price is just taking a break, not reversing.

CHAPTER 6
Recognizing Continuation Patterns in Candlestick Formations

Markets don't always reverse. In fact, most of the time, they're either moving with a trend or pausing before continuing. That pause is where continuation patterns come into play. If you can recognize these pauses, you'll stop exiting too early and start holding through stronger runs. Continuation patterns show up frequently, but they only stand out once you begin to view the market as a sequence of energy, building, releasing, and resetting.

What Continuation Patterns Represent

Continuation patterns form when the market slows down within a trend. Price takes a breather, not because the trend is ending, but because participants are waiting for more information. In real-time, these moments can feel uncertain. You might see price moving sideways or pulling back, and it's easy to assume the trend is over. That's a common mistake.

I've exited trades too early just because I didn't recognize what was happening. You may have done the same. These periods are not the end of momentum, they're usually the market reloading before making its next move.

During these moments, you'll notice candles start to contract, forming smaller bodies. Wicks may start appearing more frequently on both sides. The overall energy shifts from explosive to indecisive, but the underlying direction remains intact. Your job is to spot this moment and stay patient.

Common Bullish Continuation Candlestick Patterns

When price is trending upward, it often takes breaks. Some of the patterns you'll spot include bullish flags, bullish pennants, and bullish inside bars. These all suggest that buyers are still in control, even if price is moving sideways or slightly down.

One of the most straightforward bullish continuation patterns is the bullish inside bar. That's when a smaller candle forms entirely within the range of the previous larger bullish candle. This shows a brief pause, but not a rejection of the move.

Another pattern to pay attention to is the bullish pennant. Here, price forms a series of lower highs and higher lows in a tight, symmetrical pattern, often following a sharp bullish impulse. When price breaks out from this pattern, the trend often continues in the original direction.

Bearish Continuation Candlestick Patterns

Downtrends also pause before continuing, and these moments are filled with opportunity if you can recognize them. A common pattern is the bearish flag. It forms after a strong downward move, with price pulling back in a narrow upward channel. The pullback may be tempting to buy, but when you recognize it as a flag, you know the downtrend likely has more to go.

Another setup to pay attention to is the bearish inside bar, especially when it forms within a flag structure. It signals temporary indecision and can be a strong clue that sellers are preparing to step in again.

One key thing I've learned is not to jump into every bearish continuation just because the trend was down. You want to look for commitment. That means clean breaks, strong closes, and minimal rejection on the breakout candle.

Chart 11: Chart showing a bearish flag with a clean breakout, continuing the downtrend.

When to Trust the Continuation

The context makes the difference. You're not just looking for a flag or pennant, you're watching how it forms, where it shows up, and what kind of energy follows it. I've seen too many trades fail simply because I ignored the environment.

You're looking for continuation patterns to form after a sharp move. If the market has been ranging for hours and suddenly creates a small triangle, it's probably not a continuation. But if the move follows a clear push with strength, clean candles, no hesitation, and then starts forming a contraction, that's a different scenario.

What helps is combining these patterns with support and resistance zones, trendlines, or even Fibonacci retracement levels. The more structure backing the pattern, the stronger it usually is.

Chart 12: chart showing a bullish flag forming between key level during an ongoing uptrend.

False Continuations and How to Spot Them Early

Not every consolidation leads to a continuation. Sometimes the market fakes out. You'll see what looks like a flag, only for price to break the wrong way. When this happens, it's usually because the market was never trending with conviction to begin with.

False continuation patterns often have messy candles. Instead of clean, tight formations, you'll notice irregular wicks, overlapping bodies, or inconsistent volume. It's a warning that the market isn't committed.

I've fallen for these traps before, especially in low-volume sessions. You get a textbook pennant, the breakout starts, and within minutes, it fails completely. The key is watching for commitment and confirmation. If a breakout doesn't hold through the next couple of candles, you're better off staying flat.

Conclusion of the Chapter

Continuation patterns keep you on the right side of the market. They help you hold onto winning trades longer and avoid the urge to jump out during every small pullback. Once you train your eyes to spot them, trading becomes less stressful and more strategic.

These aren't magic patterns; they're snapshots of how traders behave when trends pause. Some will work perfectly, others will fail, but your job isn't to be perfect. It's to stay consistent, read the behavior behind the candles, and build your edge one setup at a time.

The next chapter will walk you through candlestick combinations. You'll learn how some patterns only reveal their meaning when they interact with others like a language with grammar, not just words.

CHAPTER 7
Understanding Candlestick Combinations and Market Psychology

Every single candle tells part of a story, but the real meaning often becomes clearer when you link multiple candles together. It's not just about spotting a hammer or engulfing pattern in isolation. It's how those candles interact with others, where they form, and what the market was doing right before they appeared.

When you read candlestick combinations, you start to hear the market more clearly. You begin to spot when traders are hesitant, when they're confident, and when they're caught offside.

Why Single Candles Aren't Always Enough

A single bullish candle in a downtrend doesn't always mean buyers are taking control. It could be a pause, a trap, or even a fake signal. That's why you need to pay attention to what follows. One candle might suggest strength, but if the next two or three show hesitation, that strength fades quickly.

I've made that mistake before, buying just because I saw a bullish pin bar. It looked clean, the wick was long, and price reacted off a known level. But the next candle was weak, and then the following one broke the low. That trade flipped on me fast.

So instead of relying on isolated signals, try stepping back and asking: What does this group of candles say together? Are buyers defending a level, or just reacting temporarily? Are sellers pulling back, or are they gone completely?

Common Bullish Combinations and What They Reveal

When a market shifts from indecision to strength, you'll often see a small-bodied candle, something like a spinning top, followed by a strong bullish close. That pairing tells you buyers were lurking and then stepped in confidently.

Another strong combination is the bullish engulfing sequence. Here, the second candle swallows the previous one entirely, showing a sudden surge of interest. You'll see this most clearly after a down move or during a pullback in an uptrend.

Even better is when these combinations appear near a support level or after a period of exhaustion selling. That's when you have structure and behavior aligning.

Bearish Combinations and Signs of Rejection

On the other end, bearish combinations give you a window into when buyers lose control. A frequent setup is the bearish engulfing pair, a small bullish candle overtaken by a strong bearish one. You'll often see this after price spikes or when buyers chase late.

It's more than just size. You want to watch how clean the move looks. A sharp, decisive bearish candle following an indecisive or overextended bullish move is a major clue that the market is turning. Some of the most powerful reversals I've caught came right after spotting that pattern.

There's also the three-candle reversal sequence: an indecisive candle, followed by a small push in the direction of the trend, and then a sharp rejection. It's not common, but when it happens around a known resistance level, the market usually follows through.

The Importance of Sequence and Timing

You don't just want to know what a candle looks like, you want to know when it shows up. For example, a reversal pattern that forms after a long trending move means something entirely different than the same pattern in a range.

If you've been watching a pair trend steadily for several sessions and then see a series of small-bodied candles followed by a strong reversal, you know traders are exhausted. That sequence has more weight than if those candles show up randomly.

The timing also matters in terms of session flow. A strong pattern forming at the London open or the New York overlap can carry more force than one that shows up during the quiet hours. I've seen clean engulfing patterns fail in dead market hours just because volume wasn't there.

When Combinations Lead You Wrong

There are days when even the cleanest setup doesn't work. You read the pattern right, the sequence was solid, and the breakout happened, only to reverse a few candles later.

Those situations usually boil down to context. Maybe there was news you missed. Maybe price was too close to a larger resistance level you didn't notice. Or maybe the market just didn't have enough fuel. That happens.

What you can do is build a habit of tracking not just the pattern, but the behavior around it. Ask yourself: Was the move clean? Was there follow-through? Was volume present? Was there structure to support the signal?

The more often you do this, the less you'll rely on candlestick shapes alone and the more you'll trust what the entire setup is telling you.

Final Thoughts

Reading candlestick combinations is like watching a conversation unfold between buyers and sellers. Sometimes the words are loud and aggressive, other times quiet and hesitant. But when you pay attention to how those "words" stack together, you start catching intent.

This chapter isn't about memorizing patterns. It's about developing the ability to read sequences, react appropriately, and filter signals through market context. When you do that, you begin to see trades before they're obvious.

In the next chapter, we'll take that clarity further by introducing candlestick formations at key market levels. That's where your edge sharpens, when behavior and structure align.

Chapter 8
Using Candlestick Signals at Key Market Levels

The strength of a candlestick signal grows when it lines up with an important market level. A strong reversal candle by itself might look impressive, but if it forms in the middle of nowhere, its reliability drops. That's why you should always look at where a candlestick appears before trusting what it says.

There's a huge difference between a bullish engulfing pattern in open space and one that shows up right at a well-tested support level. One is guessing. The other is context. And that context is what turns a good setup into a great trade.

Support and Resistance: The Backbone of Market Structure

You'll often hear traders talk about support and resistance, and for good reason. These are areas where price has historically reacted, either bounced or stalled. Support acts like a floor, resistance like a ceiling. If you're trading without recognizing these zones, it's like sailing without a compass.

Now, when you see a candlestick reversal at a well-defined support, it tells you that buyers are stepping in where they've stepped in before. That gives the signal more weight. The same is true for a bearish pattern that forms near resistance.

I used to trade without marking these levels, relying solely on candle shapes. Sometimes it worked, often it didn't.

Once I started pairing signals with structure, my win rate didn't just improve, my confidence grew.

Trendlines and Channels: Dynamic Guides

Not all levels are horizontal. Trendlines and price channels offer dynamic support and resistance. When price pulls back into a rising trendline and forms a bullish pattern, that's another form of confluence. You're seeing structure and behavior align.

Think of a market that's been moving upward for hours. You draw a trendline connecting the lows. Then price touches that trendline and forms a strong bullish candle. You're not just reacting to a candle. You're confirming that buyers are still in control.

The same works with channels. When price nears the edge of a descending channel and shows signs of rejection, you're being given a potential opportunity, not a guarantee, but something worth watching.

Chart 13: chart showing price respecting a rising trendline with a bullish rejection candle.

Supply and Demand Zones: Understanding Imbalance

Support and resistance can be sharpened further by identifying supply and demand zones. These are areas where a strong move originated, suggesting that an imbalance occurred. When price returns to these zones, it often reacts.

Let's say price drops hard from a level and doesn't linger. That tells you supply exceeded demand. If price later returns and stalls at that level again, forming a bearish engulfing pattern, it's likely that sellers are active again. That reaction is valuable.

Candlestick signals in these zones help you gauge whether the imbalance is still in play or if it's losing its edge.

Round Numbers and Psychological Levels

Sometimes, the levels that matter aren't from trendlines or past highs and lows. They're simply whole numbers, like 1.3000 or 1.0000. Traders tend to cluster around these psychological points, which makes reactions more likely.

When a candlestick signal appears at one of these round numbers, it's often worth paying attention to. Especially if the market is already stretched or if the number aligns with a higher timeframe zone.

A bullish candle forming off 1.0000 on EUR/USD after days of decline? That's something to track closely.

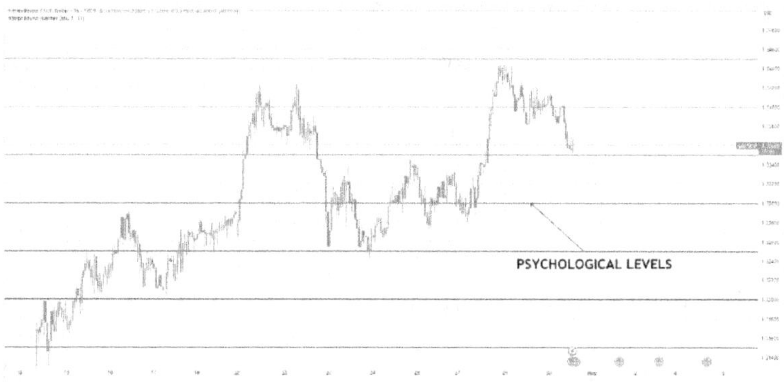

Chart 14: GBP/USD 1hour chart showing a bullish engulfing candle forming at the round number with previous support

Combining Multiple Levels for High-Quality Setups

The more layers of confirmation you add, the better your edge becomes. A reversal candle at support is useful. If it's also at the bottom of a channel, near a psychological level, and shows up during a key session, that's an opportunity with real potential.

I've had some of my cleanest trades form in those moments. You don't get them every day, and when they do appear, they don't always explode. But more often than not, the reaction is strong enough for a well-managed trade.

This doesn't mean you should clutter your charts with every possible level. Focus on the ones with the clearest price reactions in the past. Keep it clean, keep it sharp, and let candlesticks speak only when they're backed by meaningful structure.

Being Patient for the Right Setup

You won't always get the perfect combination. Some trades will tempt you to act early. But rushing into a move without clear structure leaves you exposed. The market isn't going anywhere. There will be another setup.

Waiting for candles to form at strong levels will save you frustration. You may feel like you're missing out, but what you're really doing is preserving capital and keeping your edge sharp.

Your job isn't to take every trade, it's to take the ones that make sense. Candlestick signals at key market levels help you separate the noise from what truly matters.

CHAPTER 9

Trade Entry and Exit Strategies Using Candlestick Patterns

Recognizing a reliable candlestick pattern is only half the job. The real results begin when you know how to act on that signal. Every trade needs two decisions: when to get in, and when to get out. And both decisions carry weight. Misplace either one, and even the best setup might fall apart.

You might spot a textbook bullish engulfing pattern on your chart. You wait, you're patient, and then price explodes upward, only to reverse right after you enter. That kind of experience teaches you that timing matters just as much as analysis.

Reading Confirmation Before Entry

A candlestick pattern needs context and confirmation. When a bullish pattern forms, you don't have to jump in right away. You let the candle close first. That tells you the story is complete. Then you wait for the next candle to show whether the signal has weight or not.

A common mistake is jumping in as the pattern forms. But that's like entering a room before the door opens all the way. Let the market confirm its intention. That confirmation could be a strong close above the pattern, or simply the next candle respecting the signal's direction.

Sometimes, even though a pattern looks promising, the following candles do nothing. That's hesitation. You avoid it by making sure the market commits before you do.

Choosing the Right Entry Point

Where you enter can make or break your trade. Some traders prefer market entries right after confirmation, while others wait for a retest of the pattern. Both approaches can work, but they have different risks.

If you enter immediately after confirmation, you're prioritizing momentum. That means you might catch the move early, but you could also walk into a pullback. On the other hand, if you wait for a retest, you're trading more defensively. You sacrifice a bit of early movement for better protection.

There were times when I chased momentum and paid for it. Then I started waiting for price to come back to the structure, maybe the middle of the engulfing candle or the support level below it. Those trades felt more controlled.

The entry choice depends on how aggressive or conservative you want to be, and how strong the pattern looks in its context.

Stop-Loss Placement: Protecting the Trade

Once you've decided to enter, the next move is defense. A stop-loss keeps you in the game long enough to grow. Without one, you're trading on hope.

For candlestick-based trades, a stop-loss usually goes just beyond the high or low of the signal. If it's a bullish signal, the stop can go slightly below the pattern's low. If it's bearish, just above the high. That way, you're giving the trade room, but not too much.

If the market breaks that level, it's likely that the pattern has failed, and you want out. I've been burned by moving stops or leaving them out altogether. Over time, I learned that honoring your original protection, even when it stings, builds discipline.

Take-Profit Planning: Knowing When to Exit

Exiting at the right moment is just as hard as entering. You see profit, and your instinct is to hold for more. Then the market turns. And what could have been a decent win becomes a loss. That's why having a clear profit target matters.

One method is to use recent support or resistance levels. Another is to aim for a risk-to-reward ratio like 1:2 or 1:3. If your stop-loss is 20 pips, your target might be 40 or 60. It gives you a logical frame to work within.

Some traders scale out, taking part of the profit early and letting the rest run. That's a way to manage uncertainty. I've used that strategy often, especially when the market starts to hesitate near a target. You secure part of the gain and still stay in the game.

Managing Trades as They Develop

Markets are alive. What looks good at entry can shift quickly. That's why you monitor your trades without micromanaging them. You want to watch, not interfere.

If the market moves in your favor, you can trail your stop. Move it behind structure to lock in some gain. Just avoid moving your stop too early. Give the trade space to breathe.

When I started trading, I'd cut my winners short and let losers run. It's a tough habit to break. But with experience, you start to see the value of staying in good trades longer and accepting when the market proves you wrong.

Being systematic about trade management helps you stay calm, even in fast markets. And that steadiness will show in your results over time.

CHAPTER 10

Building a Trading Routine with Candlestick Patterns

A trading strategy on its own isn't enough. You can know the patterns, understand the signals, and still find yourself making inconsistent decisions. That's where a solid trading routine comes in. It gives your strategy structure, and it helps you act based on logic instead of impulse.

Many traders underestimate this part. They're eager to trade, but they skip the preparation. I used to do that, too. I would open the charts, see something that looked good, and jump in. There wasn't any structure to what I was doing, and it showed in the results.

Setting the Right Conditions Before Trading

You don't just turn on your screen and trade. You prepare yourself mentally. The state you're in affects the decisions you make. If your head's not clear, your charts won't make sense either.

Some traders like to start with meditation. Others prefer reviewing their trading journal or watching the previous day's market replay. You need to find what puts you in a calm, focused state. That's your launch pad.

I personally start each session by scanning the major forex pairs for any significant structure, support, resistance, trendlines, and key zones. If there's no clear structure, I don't force trades. That habit alone saved me from chasing setups that weren't ready.

Marking Key Price Zones Before Market Opens

Before entering any trade, you mark out the zones where price is likely to react. These levels guide your attention and help you frame your decisions with more confidence.

Candlestick patterns near these levels carry more weight. A bullish pin bar forming at strong support, for example, isn't just a coincidence. It's a sign that buyers are stepping in at a place they've defended before.

If you don't mark these areas ahead of time, you're more likely to get distracted by patterns that occur in the middle of nowhere. And those tend to fail more often.

Having a Checklist for Trade Execution

When your setup forms, you want to be sure it meets your criteria. That's where a checklist helps. It's a short list you mentally or physically go through before entering a trade.

Does the pattern align with the trend? Is it forming at a strong level? Has the market confirmed it with a proper close? Is there room for price to move toward your target?

If the answer to any of these is no, you might wait. I've seen many good patterns that didn't meet the context. Walking away was the right choice more often than not.

The checklist keeps you objective. It makes your trades repeatable, and over time, it builds consistency. That's what separates random success from sustainable growth.

Logging Trades and Reviewing Your Journal

After you finish a trade, the work isn't over. You review what happened. Whether the trade was a win or a loss, you write it down. Entry, exit, stop-loss, target, and a few notes on what you were thinking.

I started keeping a journal after I lost three trades in a row and couldn't explain why. The journal revealed a pattern in my decision-making that I wasn't aware of. I was entering too early. Fixing that one mistake made a big difference.

Your trading journal becomes your teacher. It shows you what's working, what's not, and what habits you need to address. You don't need to write essays, just honest, clear reflections on your trades.

Ending the Day with Reflection, Not Emotion

When the trading day ends, you shut the charts, not your mind. You give yourself a few minutes to review your actions. Not just your results, but your mindset.

Were you calm? Did you follow your plan? Did you second-guess your strategy or stick with it?

Ending the day this way helps you stay grounded. It also keeps your emotions from carrying over into the next session. You don't want to trade tomorrow with the weight of today's mistakes.

It took me a while to learn this. There were days I ended frustrated, carried that into the next morning, and messed up again. But with a reflection habit, I learned to reset. That reset makes every new session a clean opportunity.

Trading isn't about doing more. It's about doing the right things repeatedly. You now have the blueprint, the patterns, the context, the entries and exits, and now the routine that ties it all together. You won't get it perfect at first, and that's okay. But if you show up every day with structure and purpose, your results will speak for themselves.

Exclusive Video Access Page

Thank you for buying my book! As a token of thanks, I've curated a collection of special video content just for you.

To get your free videos, just click the link below:

[Access Your Videos Here]

https://drive.google.com/drive/folders/1yg_Rox6b6ynEut-9hXtAZ8BaAObiWCdh?usp=drive_link

I sincerely appreciate your support, and I hope these new materials will enhance your reading experience.

Warm regards.

Nathaniel J. brooks

www.ingramcontent.com/pod-product-compliance
Lightning Source LLC
LaVergne TN
LVHW022014200926
848481LV00007B/2393
* 9 7 9 8 2 9 5 6 0 3 6 6 2 *